Contents

Introduction

Although water covers over two thirds of the Earth, only about three per cent of this water is fresh. Most is salty and lies in the oceans and seas. Over three quarters of the freshwater is frozen in the huge ice caps of the Arctic and Antarctic, and in glaciers. Most of the rest lies underground, and is called groundwater. This seems to leave very little over, yet it is enough to form mighty rivers and huge lakes, ponds, swamps and marshes all over the world.

Some 115,000 billion cubic metres of freshwater falls on our planet each year as snow or rain. All the water that falls has passed through the water cycle. The sun's heat causes the water in the sea and on land to evaporate and rise into the air as water vapour. As the air rises, it cools down and condenses into water droplets, which form clouds. A cloud is made up of billions of tiny water droplets, which crash together and get bigger until they are heavy enough to fall to Earth. The rain or snow falls back into the rivers, ponds, lakes and the sea, and the cycle starts again.

Rivers, ponds and lakes have provided people with drinking water, food and power for centuries, yet we are turning many of them into dirty dumping grounds. Industries are built on river banks so that they can use the river water. In return, they pour waste water – heavily contaminated with toxic chemicals – back into the river. Towns and cities discharge their sewage waste into rivers and lakes. Increased demand for food has led farmers to use more chemicals on their fields. The chemicals are washed off the land and into rivers and carried into

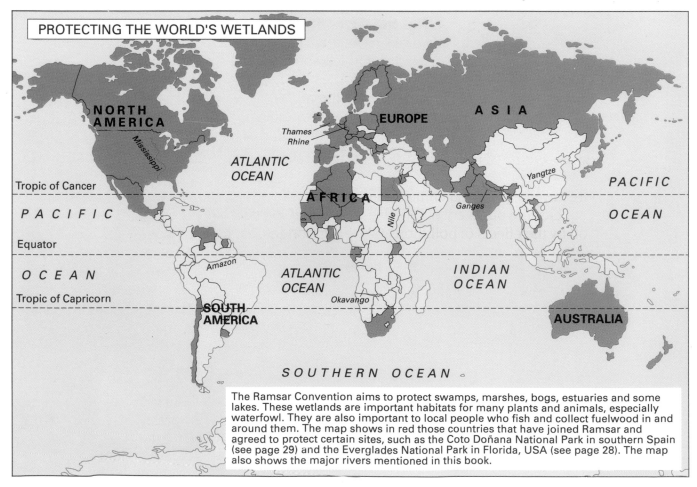

PROTECTING THE WORLD'S WETLANDS

The Ramsar Convention aims to protect swamps, marshes, bogs, estuaries and some lakes. These wetlands are important habitats for many plants and animals, especially waterfowl. They are also important to local people who fish and collect fuelwood in and around them. The map shows in red those countries that have joined Ramsar and agreed to protect certain sites, such as the Coto Doñana National Park in southern Spain (see page 29) and the Everglades National Park in Florida, USA (see page 28). The map also shows the major rivers mentioned in this book.

R...DS
...S

Anita Ganeri

Cloverleaf
An imprint of Evans Brothers Limited

Cloverleaf is an imprint of Evans Brothers Limited

Evans Brothers Limited
2A Portman Mansions
Chiltern Street
London W1M 1LE

First published 1991

Typeset by Fleetlines Typesetters, Southend-on-Sea
Printed in Spain by GRAFO, S.A. - Bilbao

ISBN 0 237 51207 6

Acknowledgements

Editor: Su Swallow
Design: Neil Sayer
Production: Jenny Mulvanny

Illustrations: David Gardner, Graeme Chambers
Maps: Hardlines, Charlbury

For permission to reproduce copyright material the author and publishers gratefully acknowledge the following:

Cover (Killarney Lakes, Ireland) Geoff Dore, Bruce Coleman Limited
Title page (Bangladesh) Mark Edwards, Still Pictures

p5 (top) Ron Cartmell, Bruce Coleman Limited, (bottom) Phillippe Henry, Oxford Scientific Films **p6** (main) Ake Lindau/Okapia, Oxford Scientific Films, (inset) Ronald Toms, Oxford Scientific Films **p7** (left) G. Ziesler, Bruce Coleman Limited, (right) Konrad Wothe, Bruce Coleman Limited **p8** NASA/Science Photo Library **p9** John Shaw, NHPA **p10** N. A. Callow, NHPA **p11** Martin Wendler, NHPA **p13** George McCarthy, Bruce Coleman Limited, (inset) Dr Eckart Pott, Bruce Coleman Limited **p14** (top) Martin Wendler, NHPA, (bottom left) David Woodfall, NHPA, (right) Michael Freeman, Bruce Coleman Limited **p15** Mark Edwards, Still Pictures **p16** Haroldo Palo, NHPA **p17** (top) Mark Edwards, Still Pictures, (bottom) Mark Carwardine, Biotica **p18** Hans Reinhard, Bruce Coleman Limited **p19** Gerald Cubitt, Bruce Coleman Limited **p20** (left) Gerald Cubitt, Bruce Coleman Limited, (right) Dieter and Mary Plage, Bruce Coleman Limited **p21** Sally Morgan/ECOSCENE **p22** Harold Taylor ABIPP, Oxford Scientific Films **p23** (top) Jane Burton, Bruce Coleman Limited, (bottom) Kim Taylor, Bruce Coleman Limited **p24** Jane Burton, Bruce Coleman Limited **p25** (top) M. P. L. Fogden, Bruce Coleman Limited, (bottom) Jane Burton, Bruce Coleman Limited **p27** Peter Hulme/ECOSCENE, (inset) Sally Morgan/ECOSCENE **p28** Jeff Foott, Bruce Coleman Limited **p29** Gordon Langsbury, Bruce Coleman Limited **p30** (top) Richard Kirby, Oxford Scientific Films, (bottom) Doug Allan, Oxford Scientific Films **p31** Peter Davey ARPS, Bruce Coleman Limited **p32** Peter Davey ARPS, Bruce Coleman Limited **p33** Jane Burton, Bruce Coleman Limited **p34** Gerald Cubitt, Bruce Coleman Limited **p35** (left) Bruce Coleman Limited, (right) Nigel Dennis NHPA **p36** (top) Jack Dermid, Oxford Scientific Films, (bottom) B. Kloske/ECOSCENE **p37** Winkley/ECOSCENE **p38** Sorensen and Olsen, NHPA **p39** (top) Mark N. Boulton, Bruce Coleman Limited, (bottom) Mark Edwards, Still Pictures **p41** Gerald Cubitt, Bruce Coleman Limited **p42** Michael Freeman, Bruce Coleman Limited **p43** D. and R. Sullivan, Bruce Coleman Limited, (inset) Sullivan and Rogers, Bruce Coleman Limited **p44** Mark Edwards, Still Pictures

△ The River Nile at Cairo

lakes and the sea, where they affect the wildlife. Some plants and animals are losing their natural habitat as wetlands are drained to provide more land for people to build or farm on.

An alarming number of freshwater plant and animal species die out every year, killed off by the effects of pollution and loss of habitat. But they are not the only ones under threat. We too rely on the same water for our most basic needs – in fact, we could not survive without it.

Compared to the oceans and the rainforests, problems in freshwater habitats do not seem to make the headlines in such a big way. However, conservation groups such as the World Wide Fund for Nature and Friends of the Earth, together with governments around the world, are working hard to put this neglect to rights. In 1975 an important step forward was taken. The Ramsar Convention came into force to protect the world's wetlands (see page 39). Some 52 countries have signed the agreement, pledging to protect and conserve over 460 wetlands (see map on page 4). Action is also being taken by local groups in many places to clean up waterways and monitor their wildlife. All the action being taken is very hopeful. But we need to do more, and keep up the pressure to safeguard our freshwater, before it is too late.

Words in **bold** are explained at the end of each section.

Grey heron

Flowing freshwater

From source to sea

Most rivers start life as bubbling springs or streams high up in the mountains. Some flow from the melting ends of glaciers. This is the river's source, the first stage on its journey to the sea. Rain and melting snow swell the stream so that it starts to flow downhill. Now it is joined by other streams, called tributaries. The area that provides a river with its water is called its drainage basin. The fast-flowing water is strong enough to transport boulders and rocks, which grind and wear away the river bed and sides. But powerful currents make the water uninhabitable for most plants, and all but the most tenacious animals.

▽ Few plants or animals inhabit the upper reaches of a river (below, in Norway) but many species thrive in the slow water of the lower reaches (inset, England).

◁ Torrent ducks can cling on in fast-flowing currents.

▽ Dippers dive to find food.

As the river leaves the hills behind, it starts to slow down. Its load is now mainly mud and sand, which grind away at its sides and broaden its valley. Plants take advantage of the slower currents and take root along the river bank. Falling leaves from riverbank trees add **nutrients** to the water, so a wider variety of animals can live in the river. The growth of plants in the river itself also increases the range of river animals which feed on them and which are in turn eaten by larger creatures, such as fish. The banks provide homes for burrowing mammals, such as otters and water voles.

As the river nears the sea, and the end of its journey, it moves at a crawl. It begins to shed its load of **sediment** which builds up its banks or washes over the surrounding plain in times of flood. The river's freshwater meets the saltwater of the sea at its mouth. Where the mouth is affected by tides, it is called an estuary. Here there may be large flocks of wading birds, gulls and other birds which can tolerate the mixture of salt and fresh water. Estuaries are also important **spawning grounds** for many fish.

Fighting the flow

Because of the speed and turbulence of the river in its upper reaches, most river animals live further downstream, where the water flows more slowly. Those that brave the swirling waters are specialists, with features designed to stop them being swept away. Some have adapted to life in both fast-flowing and slow-moving water, changing their lifestyles to suit.

Torrent ducks live high up in the racing mountain streams of the Andes, in South America. Here strong currents make life very dangerous, yet torrent ducks survive and thrive. They have streamlined bodies and webbed feet for swimming, and long tails for steering. Even more usefully, they have clawed feet which give a firm foothold on the treacherous mid-stream boulders from which the ducks dive to find food.

Another torrent specialist is the dipper. It does not have webbed feet, but is a skilful underwater hunter. The dipper swims down to the stream bed and walks along the bottom, flicking its wings to keep its balance. Thick, waterproofed feathers keep it warm as it searches for insect **larvae**, snails and tadpoles to eat. Dippers live in clear mountain streams in Europe, North and South America, North Africa and Asia.

Several members of the catfish family have special adaptations which allow them to combat the stream's flow. Some can grip and climb almost vertical rock faces, using fins converted into suckers. Others hang on with their mouths. They have large, fleshy lips for suction. A third type of catfish, called a bullhead, has a flattened body which enables it to wedge itself under stones.

7

△ The Nile has a fan-shaped delta with a fairly smooth coastline.

The journey's end

Around the mouths of many of the world's greatest rivers, new land is formed as the river deposits its load of mud and sand sediment. This is called a delta. The river is forced to branch out in order to flow around the piles of sediment. If the area is not affected by strong tides, the delta gradually builds up, pushing the coastline further out to sea. Deltas laced by small streams, or distributaries, are fan-shaped or shaped like birds' feet.

The mighty Mississippi River of the United States enters the sea through a huge, birds-foot delta in the Gulf of Mexico. The river carries an enormous load of mud and sand towards its delta – some 500 million tonnes each year. Some of this sediment is deposited on the river's flood plains, enriching the soil and making fertile fields for growing cotton. But people living along the river build barriers to protect them from the river's flood waters, so these fertile plains are being destroyed. The river is forced to carry its whole load of sediment

down to its delta. Whilst the delta is expanding at an amazing 60m a year, the flood plains are gradually sinking. With them go huge areas of valuable farmland.

The delta of the River Nile in Egypt is also important for farming and is also under threat. The combination of water and rich sediment deposits led the Ancient Egyptians to found their civilisation in the area around the Nile delta over 5,000 years ago. They found the land excellent for growing crops such as barley, dates, grapes and wheat.

Today, however, this delta is fast losing its fertility, and river water is being diverted. The problems have been caused by the building of a series of large hydroelectric dams for producing electricity. They include the huge Aswan Dam, which holds the river water back in a great man-made reservoir, Lake Nasser. The 100 million tonnes of mud that would normally have fertilised the delta is now silting up the lake instead. Instead of being built forward into the sea, the delta is in fact being worn away by the waves.

One of the casualties of the plight of the

Nile delta is the papyrus plant. It is now officially classed as endangered in Egypt. In Ancient Egypt, papyrus was used to make mats, paper and sails, and was adopted as a royal symbol. Today, as water is taken from the Nile, the swamps and ponds around the delta are either drying up altogether or being made saltier by the incoming sea water. The papyrus is struggling to survive these changes to its habitat. Its loss will deprive people of a valuable source of fuel. Papyrus can grow very fast and a small area can produce a huge number of plants. Local people collect the plants and compress them into papyrus logs, which can be burnt for heat and cooking.

Papyrus

Intrepid travellers

Rivers not only provide permanent homes for many creatures, but are also used as journey routes for others, in particular salmon and eels. These fish lead a double life, spending part of their lives as sea fish and part as freshwater fish. Birds are perhaps the animals best known for their long journeys, called migrations, to find food or a warmer climate. But salmon and eels also display remarkable endurance and navigation skills, as they swim between the rivers and the sea.

Leaping salmon

Female salmon lay their eggs in a scooped out hollow in the gravel on the bed of a fast-flowing stream. As many as 14,000 eggs may be laid at one time. Then the eggs are covered with sand so they are not swept away by the current. The young salmon which hatches from the egg is called an alevin. It still carries part of its yolk-sac with it for food, until it becomes a fry which can find food for itself. The salmon then spends another two to three years as a parr feeding in the river before it becomes a silvery smolt. At this stage, the smolt starts its journey to the sea. After about four years at sea, the salmon makes the journey back up the rivers to spawn. Pacific salmon face a journey of many thousands of kilometres, and cover about 115km a day. They swim upstream, against the current, leaping

▽ Salmon can leap over waterfalls.

several metres over any waterfalls in their path. Amazingly, the salmon are able to find the very stream where they themselves were born. Scientists think that they find their way by following the smell of a particular river. The smell is made up of chemicals dissolved in the water, which come from rocks, soil and vegetation.

Most salmon die after spawning. Unfortunately, many are also killed by pollution in the water before they reach the sea. Rivers in Norway, Wales and Scotland have lost their salmon because of pollution. Acid rain has killed the salmon in ten or more rivers in Nova Scotia in Canada. Other modern hazards are dams, locks and weirs. These block the salmon's path, and the fish get lost. In some rivers, salmon ladders have been built to ease the fish's journey upriver. The salmon can swim up the ladders in easy stages, without losing their way. This system, together with programmes to clean up the water, has already led to salmon returning to some American rivers after many years' absence. Salmon disappeared from White River, USA, about 100 years ago. They have now returned after a ten-year cleaning-up programme.

Eel marathons

European and North American eels, like the salmon, divide their lives between the sea and rivers. They spend most of their lives in a river, until the time comes to breed. Then they swim downriver and out to the Sargasso Sea, a huge area of calm water in the North Atlantic. The eels lay their eggs, then die.

Soon the young eels, though only about 8cm long, start out on their incredible journey back to the river in which their parents lived. The European eel takes about three years to cover the 6,000km to the rivers of Europe. The eels are carried eastward by the powerful Gulf Stream current. The journey to North America is shorter, about 1,600km, and takes the eels about one year. Each type of eel grows at a different rate and they are about the same size when they reach their destinations. They live in the rivers for about 15 years. Then they swim back to the Sargasso Sea, to spawn and die.

△ Dye from a factory has polluted this river in Austria.

River pollution

Animal and plant life in rivers all over the world is dying because of the huge amounts of refuse, poisonous chemicals, toxic waste and sewage effluent pumped into them each day (see also page 36). The River Vistula in Poland, for example, is so polluted that its water is completely unusable for most of its 1,068km length. It is one of the rivers that flows into the Baltic Sea, where its pollution spreads right across the water to Sweden. As a result of such pollution, the number of grey seals in the Baltic has dropped dramatically from about 100,000 to just 2,000 since the beginning of this century. The Vistula is not alone. Many rivers have become little more than open sewers, too polluted to sustain fish or any living creatures.

Agricultural run-off – substances that run off the land into nearby freshwater – is a major source of river pollution. The use of chemical pesticides and fertilisers on farmland worldwide is increasing by over 12 per cent each year. Rain washes more than half the pesticide off the land and into rivers and groundwater, where it poisons river water.

The DDT danger

One of the worst agricultural poisons that finds its way into rivers is the pesticide DDT. It is effective and easy to use as it remains active for many years. But in the 1950s scientists became aware that there was a link between DDT and eggshell thinning in

△ Otters die when they eat fish poisoned by pollution in rivers.

birds and the death of birds of prey. So DDT was banned, though it is still used illegally, and used in poorer countries where cheap alternatives are not available.

DDT can kill insects, but the poison is stored in their bodies so that, if they are eaten by fish or birds, for example, it is passed on and up the food chain. Each time it passes from one animal to another, the poison becomes more concentrated. So in birds of prey, badgers and foxes at the top of the food chain, the poison is many thousands of times stronger than when it was first sprayed on the fields. In Europe, the ban came just in time to save peregrines and bald eagles from extinction, but other predators in developing countries may be in danger from DDT.

Another pesticide, dieldrin, has also caused serious problems. It too is washed off farmland and into rivers where it poisons the fish and animals such as otters which feed on the fish. Like DDT, dieldrin does not break down, but becomes more concentrated as it passes up the food chain. In certain rivers, fish have been so contaminated with dieldrin that otters are today in great danger in the wild. Despite a ban on the pesticide in North America and Europe, a 1985 survey showed that otters in these places were still being killed by eating poisoned fish.

In shallow water, beavers build a dam of logs across the river to create a pool of shallow still water. They use their strong teeth to fell trees and cut them into logs. Beavers raise their young and store food in a lodge, which they build in the pool out of branches and twigs.

Other offenders

Industrial pollution now accounts for nearly 40 per cent of all water pollution incidents. Heavy metals, such as cadmium, copper, lead, nickel, mercury and zinc, are among the worst offenders. Waste from the manufacturing processes contains small amounts of heavy metals, which find their way into the river water. Even in very low doses they can be lethal to wildlife. PCBs (polychlorinated biphenols), used in the plastics industry, are another ingredient in the toxic soup. Some countries, especially in North America and Europe, now have strict regulations to control the amount of dangerous chemicals that industries can discharge into rivers.

Sadly, even messing about on the river adds to the threat of pollution. Angling is a popular sport and most anglers are responsible and caring for the environment. However, in Great Britain alone over 10,000 mute swans are killed each year by swallowing lead fishing weights. In the USA, thousands of mallard ducks are poisoned after eating similar weights.

River care

We often take our rivers for granted. But as we have seen, rivers and their wildlife are under attack from all sides. The water is being polluted so much that fish can no longer survive. Animals that have lived by rivers for thousands of years are losing their habitats as more and more land is used for building or farming. Unless we start taking better care of these freshwater habitats, they will quickly become nothing but dirty stretches of water, with none of the wildlife or character that makes them special.

▷ Swans (inset) die from eating lead weights used by fishermen (main picture).

nutrients – food substances used by living things for growth and energy.
sediment – mud, sand or fine soil carried by a river.
spawning grounds – the place where animals such as fish lay their eggs.
larvae – young form of some insects, which is quite different from the adult.

Rivers around the world

There are rivers all over the world, high up in the mountains, in the steamy hot tropics and even in deserts. They are home to a remarkable range of plants and animals, from gigantic snakes to antelopes, and from huge water lilies to great forests of mangroves. They also provide a source of food and water for many people, and are symbols of luck to others. Sadly, it is people who are spoiling them.

The mighty Amazon

The Amazon is the world's second longest river, next to the River Nile. From its source high up in the snow-capped Andes mountains in Peru, it flows some 6,437km across South America to enter the Atlantic Ocean at its delta in northern Brazil. In the Amazon's early stages, over 50 tributaries flow into the river.

The river drains almost half of South America, an area equivalent to the size of Australia. A great deal of the drainage basin is made up of hot, tropical rainforest, where rain falls almost every day. As a result, the Amazon carries more water than any other

△ The anaconda squeezes its prey (such as caimans) to death, then swallows them whole.

△ The piranha (above), with its razor-sharp teeth, is the most ferocious fish in the Amazon (left).

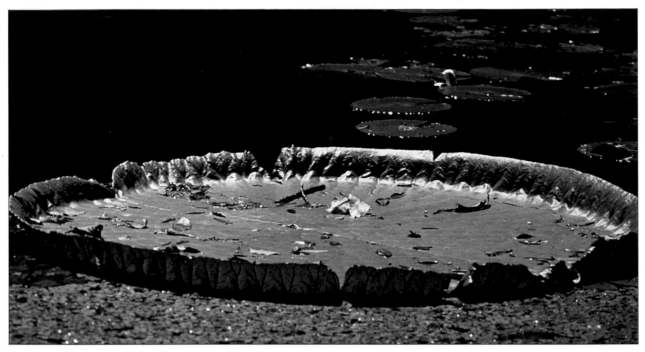

△ The Amazonian water lily has giant leaves.

river on Earth. At any one time, about two thirds of all the freshwater in the world is flowing down the Amazon. At its delta, the river pours into the ocean with such power that the water is still fresh 160km out to sea.

Animal attack

Tropical rivers are home to a wide variety of fish. Among the 2,000 fish species living in the Amazon, the most ferocious is the piranha.

Piranhas are fairly small fish, no more than 60cm long. But they have razor-sharp, triangular teeth, so sharp in fact, that the Amazonian Indians use them as scissors and knives. The piranhas attack in shoals, becoming ever more frenzied as they feed. A shoal of these fiercesome predators can strip a cow to its bones in just a few minutes. Their normal prey, though, consists of dead or injured fish.

Animals that visit the river to drink, such as horses, deer and tapir risk being attacked not only by piranhas, but by other river creatures. The anaconda, or water boa, is the heaviest snake in the world, and one of the longest. It can weigh 200kg and reach 9m in length. The snake is largely aquatic, spending most of its life in the water, where it preys on animals as large as pigs and caimans. It squeezes them to death, then swallows them whole. The anaconda is an excellent swimmer, but it can also climb well to shelter in trees along the river banks.

Lily plates

One of the most spectacular river plants is the giant Amazonian water lily. Its huge pads can be over 1.5m across, among the largest leaves of any plant in the world. An upturned rim prevents the leaves becoming waterlogged, whilst thick, air-filled ribs underneath the leaves keep them buoyant. These ribs give such firm reinforcement that a lily pad is strong enough to bear the weight of a child.

Water lilies are found in many lakes and slow-moving rivers around the world. Their rubbery stems are firmly anchored in the mud on the bottom. Their leaves and flowers float on the surface. Water snails lay their eggs under the lily leaves, although some leaves have sharp prickles to deter them. Frogs rest on or under the leaves, and fish take advantage of the shade they provide. Water lily flowers follow a regular daily routine. They are closed in the morning, open out at about midday, and close again towards nightfall. This may be a ploy to attract the insects that pollinate the flowers, and are more active in the warmth of the middle of the day.

▽ Amazonian manatee

Manatee management

Manatees are large, lumbering aquatic mammals. One type, the Amazonian manatee, lives only in the River Amazon. It cannot tolerate salt water, unlike other manatees which live along tropical coasts. In the past the docile Amazonian manatees have been killed in their thousands for their meat. They are a threatened species, now protected by an international agreement, known as CITES (Convention on International Trade in Endangered Species of Flora and Fauna).

Manatees are herbivores, browsing on floating and submerged river plants. Their feeding habits may help them to survive. In 1976 a study of manatees was started by the National Research Institute for the Amazon. In one conservation project, manatees were used to control, naturally, the growth of floating weed in man-made reservoirs and hydroelectric dams. The weed grows rapidly, clogging up the electricity turbines and stopping light entering the water. The lack of light kills off plant plankton, the food of many fish, which then die. The manatees eat the weeds, and wildlife and machinery benefit from the clearer water. The manatees also excrete nutrients into the water. The plankton thrives on these extra nutrients, and in turn provides more food for the fish.

Amazon in danger

The greatest threat to the River Amazon is the destruction of the tropical rainforest which grows along its banks. An area of rainforest the size of Austria is cut down each year. This disturbs the balance of the drainage basin. Soil on the forest floor is no longer anchored down by tree roots, and the rain washes it into the river. In some places, the water is so muddy it is difficult to see more than a few centimetres ahead.

There are vast mineral reserves in the area, with rich stores of gold, uranium and iron ore. Huge gold mining programmes have brought thousands of prospectors to the area, with heavy machinery for extracting the gold. The pollution caused by all these activities is poisoning the river and its wildlife. Mercury is used, illegally, in the processing of gold and thousands of tonnes of mercury alone are poured into the water.

Today, conservation groups are trying to persuade governments in South America to preserve the rainforests. If they are successful, the river and its extraordinary wildlife are assured of a future.

The sacred Ganges

India's main river, the Ganges, rises in the Himalayan mountains and flows about 2,500km eastwards to join the Brahmaputra River in Bangladesh. The two rivers then continue through a huge delta into the Bay of Bengal and the Indian Ocean. The river is considered sacred by Hindus. They believe that bathing in the river will cleanse them of their sins. Among the holy sites on its banks are the cities of Varanasi and Allahabad, where great numbers of pilgrims gather to bathe and to pray. People also believe that it is lucky to die on the banks of the Ganges, and that this will make their journey to heaven shorter. Bodies are cremated (burnt) on the river banks, and the ashes scattered on the water. Water from the Ganges is also used for irrigation in India and Bangladesh.

Pollution problems

Many of the cities along the banks of the Ganges, including Varanasi, have no treatment plants for sewage. So human, and

animal, wastes find their way straight into the water. Adding to the problem are increasingly large amounts of toxic and chemical wastes being pumped into the river from agriculture and industry. As a result large stretches of the river are like an open sewer. Some 600km of its length are so polluted that it is considered dangerous to health. The problem, of course, does not stop there. The pollution is carried from the cities into the countryside and eventually into the sea.

In an attempt to restore life to the river, the Indian government has put aside over £4 million to be used in a five-year clean-up campaign. The project will involve building new sewage treatment plants and controlling the use of chemical fertilisers.

This project may also help to save the river dolphins, which are seriously threatened by the pollution in the Ganges. There are only five species of river dolphin in the world. Two species live in South America, one in the Yangtze River, China, and one each in

△ Pilgrims visit the Ganges to bathe and pray.
▽ Boat traffic on the Yangtze River, China, threatens the survival of the Baiji dolphin. (right).

the Ganges and the Indus rivers. Everywhere they are under increasing threat as their habitats are destroyed. In the Indus River, the construction of dams to provide water for irrigation and power has severely restricted the movement of the dolphins and the fish they feed on. The Ganges dolphin is slightly better off, although its survival is by no means guaranteed. The most threatened species of all is the Baiji dolphin of the Yangtze River. The river is China's main commercial highway, and the noise from river traffic interferes with the dolphin's echo-location (see below). Its sense of direction becomes confused and many dolphins are hit by boats or injured by their propellers. Others become entangled in fishing nets or are poisoned by pollution.

The Baiji dolphin was not discovered until 1914. Today there are fewer than 400 left in the Yangtze, and the dolphin faces extinction. A huge project to build special reserves for them on the river itself is almost complete. This may be the last chance to save these extraordinary creatures.

Swimming in the dark

River dolphins use echo-location to navigate underwater. They emit series of very high-pitched clicks by forcing air through passages in their heads. The sound is focused into a beam by a special organ in the dolphin's head, called the melon. It is this organ which gives the dolphin's forehead its characteristic dome shape. The beam scans the water ahead. If it hits a solid object, it sends back an echo. River dolphins have excellent hearing. From the echo they receive, they can tell how far away the object is and even distinguish between objects such as rocks or plants.

This system is so effective that the dolphins have no real use for their eyes. The eyes of the Ganges river dolphins are tiny and do not even have lenses. They are only strong enough to tell whether it is night or day.

Mangrove forest
The biggest mangrove forest in the world, the Sundarbans, stretches almost 6,000km across the Ganges and Brahmaputra delta. Mangroves form an unusual and valuable ecosystem. They are essential spawning grounds for fish and shellfish and in turn, a rich harvest for people. About 80 per cent of India's fish catch comes from this area. The mangroves also help protect the Indian and Bangladeshi coasts from the frequent tropical storms.

The Sundarbans were set up as a reserve for the Royal Bengal tiger. As with mangrove swamps all over the world, though, they are under threat. About 1,550 sq km of mangroves have been cut down in the last 100 years. Large areas have also been drained to make land for building and for industry. The area is also exploited for its stocks of firewood, timber and fish. After terrible storms and flooding in 1970, caused partly by the loss of the mangroves' protection, the government of Bangladesh planted a further 25,000 hectares of trees.

△ Tigers are protected in the Sundarbans.

Flood alert
In common with many deltas, the Ganges delta has created a huge plain of fertile land. Land is very precious in Bangladesh. Most people there are very poor, and many farm their crops on the delta to earn their living.

However, the plain is low-lying and frequently hit by devastating floods and tropical cyclones. In 1970, a year of record floods, as many as 300,000 people were killed by the combination of flood water and huge waves driven inland by cyclones. In 1990 at least 200,000 people drowned.

△ Swamps in the Okavango Delta

The frequency of such catastrophes is increasing. The destruction of mangrove swamps makes the coast more vulnerable to attack from the sea. Cutting down forests high up in the Himalayas affects the river much further down its course. The loss of tree cover allows heavy monsoon rain to strip soil from the hillsides. The soil raises the river's bed, increasing the likelihood of flooding. As a result, over 45,000 Indian villages a year are flooded during the heavy monsoon rains.

The Okavango Delta

The River Okavango in Africa flows south from the Angolan highlands into northern Botswana. However, unlike the majority of the world's rivers, it does not flow into the sea but sinks into the sands of the Kalahari Desert, forming a huge, fan-shaped, inland delta. It is unique because it is a purely freshwater delta, not affected by the sea. In the delta the river divides up into thousands of tributaries and streams, dotted with lagoons and small islands.

19

Each year, in the dry season, the delta floods. Although most of the rain which falls on the area evaporates away, the river is swollen by rainwater carried from the highlands, which takes five months to reach the delta. In some years, floodwaters spread the delta over 22,000 sq km of the Kalahari.

Animals of the Okavango

The Okavango Delta provides a huge, varied habitat for an enormous variety of animals, from storks and cormorants to crocodiles and lions. Many animals take refuge in the papyrus swamps of the upper delta, whilst birds, such as fish eagles, inhabit the clear waters and lagoons. The millions of islands in the delta provide feeding and nesting sites for ibis and other birds.

During the day, Pel's fishing owl, a nocturnal hunter, roosts in the fig trees which line the banks of the delta. As night falls, it leaves its roost and perches in wait on a low branch overhanging the river. As soon as it spots a fish, it drops into the water, feet first, and scoops up its prey. The owl has huge eyes for seeing in the dark and spines on its feet to help it grip its prey, such as catfish.

The swamp antelope, or sitatunga, lives and feeds in the delta's swampy papyrus reedbeds. It has several adaptations to help it survive in this habitat. It is able to live on a diet of papyrus and its large hooves splay out as it walks, so it can cross marshy ground without sinking. If threatened, the swamp antelope may submerge itself in the water, with just its nostrils showing, until the danger has passed.

Many of the smaller islands in the delta are dominated by termite mounds, built by tiny termite insects out of clay and their own saliva. The mounds are important nesting sites for kingfishers and other birds. The tiny malachite kingfisher starts looking for a mate in October, tempting the female with gifts of pieces of fish. Then the two birds dig their nest together, often in the side of a termite mound. The female lays four to six eggs. Then the parents share the task of looking after the eggs and finding food for the newly-hatched chicks.

Okavango under threat

In December 1990, plans were revealed to drain part of the delta to supply water to the Orapa mine, the world's largest diamond mine. The government of Botswana, together with a private company, wanted to dredge a large section of the Boro River, the

◁ Pel's fishing owl
▷ Malachite kingfisher

20

Okavango's main channel. Many conservation groups, including Greenpeace, set about trying to stop the development, which would turn a large part of the delta into desert.

While the bulldozers stood ready to start work, Greenpeace threatened to launch an international campaign, called 'Diamonds are for death'. The government was seriously worried about what this bad publicity would mean to the country's diamond industry which brings in most of its money. However, it was protests from local tribespeople that finally brought work to a halt in March 1991. Many of them survive by fishing in the delta, gathering edible water plants and collecting reeds for thatching huts. They also use palms from the delta to weave baskets which they sell to local tourists and abroad. Without the delta, their survival, as well as that of the wildlife, would be threatened. Their protest seemed to do the trick. For the time being, the delta is safe. The developers' plans have not been shelved, but they have been put on hold, hopefully for ever.

Tale of two rivers

The River Rhine

The River Rhine is Europe's chief river and thoroughfare, and passes through Liechtenstein, Austria, Germany, France and the Netherlands. The Rhine flows through some of the most heavily industrialised regions in the world. Mines, factories and farms pollute its water with heavy metals, sewage, and chlorine.

In 1986, fire broke out at a chemical factory near Basel, Switzerland. Over 30 tonnes of poisonous chemicals, including pesticides, dyes and fungicides, poured into the Rhine, causing widespread pollution. A 3,204km stretch of the river was rendered lifeless and half a million fish were killed.

Steps have now been taken to improve the quality of the river water and allow fish to flourish in it once more. However, levels of nitrates in the river are almost at the maximum level set by the World Health Organisation as being safe. There are fears that nitrate-contaminated drinking water causes cancer.

The River Thames

The River Thames flows for about 340km from the Cotswold Hills, through the centre of London and into a long estuary which leads to the North Sea.

By the late 1950s large stretches of the river were almost dead. The water had become black and smelly because of heavy pollution. In 1963, the estuary had become uninhabitable for fish. Today there are over 100 kinds of fish in it, thanks to an extensive clean-up campaign.

Over the last 30 years pollution control carried out by several authorities has brought the river back to life. Sewage systems have been updated. Oil spilled on the river has been sprayed with chemicals to clean it off. Salmon have now returned, together with other migratory fish.

Today the health of the river is closely monitored by the National Rivers Authority.

Worldwide problem

Rivers in different countries face different problems, but they share the growing threat of pollution. With international and local pressure increasing all the time, it does seem that governments are at last taking notice of people's fears and that efforts are now being made to clean up and protect rivers around the world.

▽ Industry on the River Rhine in Germany

Wetlands or wastelands?

△ Mallard ducks often nest beside ponds.

Ponds, swamps, marshes and bogs are among the richest habitats on Earth. They produce more plant matter than the most fertile grasslands, and are home to thousands of animals. Sadly, they are often considered to be wastelands and as a result are under great threat wherever they occur. Rubbish is dumped in them, they are drained or filled in to create dry land, and they are poisoned by pollution.

The pond community

A pond is a good example of an ecosystem, a largely self-contained unit made up of the relationships between the pond habitat, its community and the world around it.

A huge number of tiny **crustaceans** and insects live in a pond. Some, such as water fleas, are able to colonise the many **microhabitats** offered by the pond. They include plant stems and leaves, the space between grains of sand and the underside of stones and rocks. The ooze of mud on the pond's bottom is home to burrowing insect larvae, mussels and other shellfish, and worms. They are among many creatures that feed on decaying plant matter which falls from the surface.

Plant zones

The plants in the pond community are divided into zones. Marginal plants, such as irises, marsh marigolds and rushes, grow around the edges of the pond. They provide shelter and food for many pond animals. If these plants are not controlled, though, they can spread rapidly and quicken the process by which ponds turn into marshland.

Floating plants such as water lilies are truly aquatic and need water to survive. They are rooted in the mud of the pond bottom and their leaves float on the surface. The leaves provide cover for many creatures. If their growth is not controlled, they can block sunlight from the water and disturb the balance of the pond. Plants need sunlight for **photosynthesis**.

Submerged plants grow near the middle of the pond. They include water milfoils and pond weeds. These plants too are rooted in the mud but, unlike floating plants, they usually grow totally underwater. They provide shelter, food and egg-laying sites. They also produce oxygen, which all living things need to breathe, and which dissolves in the water. Free-floating plants, such as duckweeds and bladderworts, are not rooted in the bottom mud. They float on, or just under, the surface often forming a thick, green blanket over the pond. Once again, their leaves and stems provide hiding places, shade and food for many pond creatures. Bladderworts are carnivorous plants. The tiny 'bladders' on their leaves have an opening at one end, closed by a trap door and surrounded with sensitive bristles. If an insect brushes against the bristles, the trap door swings open and the animal is sucked inside and slowly digested.

Algae, the simplest type of plants, are found in sea and fresh water. Most pond algae are no bigger than full stops; many can only be seen under a microscope.

They can multiply very quickly in warm weather, turning the water green (see page 36).

Plants not only provide the pond with essential oxygen, but, because of their ability to produce their own food, provide the first link in the pond's food chain. They are eaten by insect larvae and tadpoles, for example, which in turn feed frogs, toads and fish. These are preyed on by herons, shrews and fishing bats, which may be caught by birds of prey. There are many different food chains in a pond, all dependent on plants. They join together to make a more complicated food web. Another essential element in the pond's food system is the decomposers. These are the fungi and bacteria which convert rotting leaves and plants back into nutrients for the animals.

From egg to adult

Some animals start life in the pond, but leave the water when they become adults. They go through an amazing transformation, changing from eggs to adult animals. This change is called metamorphosis.

A dragonfly starts life as an egg laid in the water. Then it changes completely before emerging as an adult. The egg hatches into a larva, or nymph. A nymph moults (sheds its skin) up to 15 times in the two years it spends growing. Then the nymph crawls up a plant stem to the surface of the pond. It moults for the final time and emerges as an adult dragonfly. This usually happens at nightfall or dawn, when there is less risk of being attacked.

A dragonfly nymph is one of the fiercest predators in the pond, crawling along the bottom in search of other insects and even small fish. It uses camouflage and stealth to catch its prey. Nymphs may be grey, brown or green. Some can change colour slightly to blend in with a particular background. As an adult, the dragonfly continues to prey on other creatures. Dragonflies are superb fliers

△ This southern aeshna dragonfly has just emerged from its nymph case.

▽ The bladderwort feeds on tiny water animals.

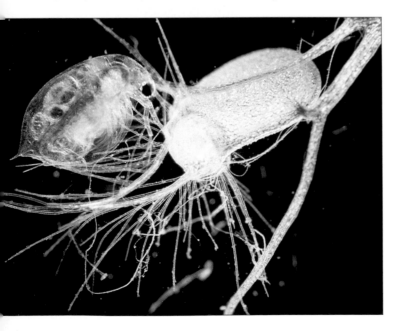

and skilful hunters. They swoop over the pond, snapping up any insects in their path. Some species can fly at up to 30km per hour. They have huge, compound eyes to spy out food as they speed over the water.

There are over 5,000 different types of dragonflies and damselflies, their close relations. They first appeared on Earth about 300 million years ago. Prehistoric dragonflies were huge. The dragonfly *Meganeura* was the biggest insect that has ever lived, with a wingspan of over 76 cm. Apart from becoming smaller, dragonflies have not changed since prehistoric times. They have survived so well by adapting to eating different sorts of insects, as the world around them has changed.

Wetland specialists

The water spider is unique among spiders because it spends its whole life in the water. It has an ingenious way of ensuring a constant supply of air. It spins a layer of silk between the stems of submerged plants. Then it goes to the surface and traps bubbles of air on its body hairs. The bubbles are released under the silk layer and more silk is added to make a bell-shaped web. Inside this diving bell there is space for the spider to feed, mate and lay its eggs. When the oxygen supply runs low, the spider visits the

▽ The water spider lives in a bubble of air inside a web.

surface again for fresh supplies.

Apart from collecting air, the spider only leaves its bell to hunt for insects and fish. These are eaten inside the bell. As winter approaches, the spider leaves its bell and goes deeper in the water. It seals itself inside another, stronger bell and hibernates until the spring.

Amphibians are specialised wetland residents, spending half their life on land and half in the water. Female frogs, for example, lay their eggs in the water where they hatch into tadpoles with bodies designed for swimming, and fish-like gills for breathing. However, as the tadpoles grow they develop lungs and legs in preparation for their adult life as land-dwellers. Even on land, though, amphibians are dependent on water and never stray far from it, or the damp ground around it. They not only breathe through their lungs, but also absorb oxygen through their skins. Dry skin does not take in oxygen, so the amphibians have to keep their bodies damp.

Some African frogs lay their eggs in trees and have ingenious means of keeping the spawn moist. African grey tree frogs mate on branches overhanging the water. Then the female produces a liquid which she and the male whisk into a frothy lather with their back legs. She lays her eggs in this foam nest, where they are kept moist. The outside of the nest soon hardens in the warm sun, trapping the moisture inside. When the eggs hatch into tadpoles, the bottom part of the nest turns to liquid again, and the tadpoles drop out of the foam into the water below.

The axolotl, a type of salamander, is one of the most unusual amphibians. It spends its whole life as a tadpole in the water, never reaching adulthood but growing up to 25cm long. It even breeds as a tadpole. Scientists discovered that these creatures need the chemical iodine to develop into mature adults. This chemical is lacking in their natural habitat. However, if the axolotl is given the chemical it needs, it loses its gills, grows legs and turns into a creature very much like a burrowing salamander.

Among the best adapted wetland animals are the lungfish. One species in Africa lives

△ Grey tree frogs make a foam nest.

◁ The axolotl is amphibious, but never leaves the water.

in pools surrounded by swamp land. In the wet season, when there is plenty of water, the lungfish lives like a normal fish, breathing through its gills. However, in the dry season, the sun dries up these pools and the water's oxygen supply disappears.

As the water level falls, the fish burrows down into the damp mud. It blocks the entrance of its tube-like burrow with a lump of mud, seals itself into a slimy, mucus cocoon and goes into a type of hibernation. During this time, the fish breathes by taking air into two pouches on its underside. These are lined with very thick blood vessels which absorb oxygen. In effect they are like very simple lungs, and are the fish's lifeline. Air passes through the mud stopper, down the burrow, into the fish's mouth and into these lungs.

The lungfish can survive in this way until the rains come and refill the pool. This may be a period of several months, or even years.

Skimming on the surface

Water is covered with an elastic-like skin. Many insects make use of this surface film to walk on water. The pond skater, for example, has thick pads of wax-covered hair on its four back legs which repel water so the skater does not sink. They also trap air so it can skim over the water. Tiny hooked claws on its feet give the skater a firm grip on the water without breaking the skin.

The pond skater uses its very back legs for steering as it 'rows' over the water with its middle pair of legs. It grabs food with its short front legs. These hunters feed on dead or dying insects which fall on to the water.

Camphor beetles, too, use the water's surface film, to escape from predators. These beetles are usually found at the water's edge, but sometimes fall into the water and run the risk of being eaten by other insects. If this happens, they eject a special chemical from their abdomens which breaks the surface film, and the beetles shoot across the water at high speed until they reach the safety of the shore again.

Marshes, swamps and peat bogs

Swamps and marshes are the in-between stages as a pond gradually turns into dry land. This happens when a pond is overwhelmed by the plants growing on its edges, such as papyrus, sawgrass and reeds. The plants' thick roots grow through the muddy ground and up into the water, where they send up new shoots and slow down the water flow. Falling leaves from waterside trees increase the tangle of vegetation. Gradually, the accumulation of plant matter and sediment turns the open water first to marsh, then to dry land in a process known as ecological succession.

These midway habitats support a wide range of wildlife. Birds such as bitterns and reed warblers are totally at home among the reed stems, where they feed on insects and hide from predators, and build their nests out of reeds.

Marshes and swamps also act as natural water purifiers, soaking up harmful chemicals from the water. They help to prevent flooding by absorbing water like sponges, and absorbing potentially damaging amounts of carbon dioxide gas from the air. The wetlands are among the most productive habitats on Earth. Some can produce over 50 times as much plant material as a similar area of grassland.

Peat bogs form in a similar way to swamps and marshes, as bog mosses take over the water. These mosses, also called sphagnum moss, can soak up ten times their own weight in water. When sphagnum dies, it does not decompose (rot) completely because of the waterlogged conditions. Instead it builds up in layers and forms peat. A peat bog may take over 5,000 years to form. If left undisturbed, it would eventually turn into coal. In the meantime, the bog provides a home for many types of plants, including pennyworts, bog pimpernels and insect-eating butterworts.

In Ireland, where plentiful rainfall and a low rate of evaporation have formed extensive bogs, peat has long been collected and used as fuel. Many ancient bogs have been destroyed in this way. Peat is also widely used in gardens to improve the growth of plants. About 90 million tonnes of peat are dug up each year, representing many thousands of years of growth and impossible to replace. Conservationists are now trying to protect the remaining bogs by encouraging people to use alternatives to peat, such as compost and farm manure.

Wetlands in peril

It is estimated that as many as half the world's wetlands have already been destroyed. Ponds have been filled in or used as rubbish tips. Marshes and swamps are drained so that the land can be reclaimed for farms or buildings. Wetlands are also flooded to provide water for drinking and irrigation.

In the USA, almost half the country's wetlands have been turned into farmland, including the famous Florida Everglades. The number of birds using these swamps

▷ Bog asphodel (inset) thrives in peat bogs such as this one in Scotland.

has fallen from about 2.5 million to 250,000 in the last 100 years. There is now a huge campaign, initiated by the state of Florida, to bring the Everglades back to life. The Everglades are part of a natural system of waterways which includes the Kissimmee River and Lake Okeechobee. Until the beginning of this century the system provided water for the swamps and for drinking. Since then, however, the swamps have been drained and dredged to provide farmers with water for their fields, and the lake has been polluted with agricultural run-off. This has greatly affected the area's unique wildlife. The run-off contains huge amounts of phosphates and nitrates. The swamps' natural sawgrass is struggling to survive in the polluted water. Its place is being taken by plants called cattails. These grow very tall, choking the swamps and blocking out sunlight. Another endangered species is the wood stork. In the last 25 years, numbers have dropped by 80 per cent.

The destruction of the Everglades not only affects wildlife, but also the people who rely on it for their living. Farmers welcomed the drainage of the swamps because of the extra water it would give them to irrigate their crops. They also found that the rich swamp soil was extremely fertile for crops. However, this soil dries out in the air once it is deprived of its water supply. It then blows away, leaving useless areas of dusty land. According to a recent survey, much of the farmland in the area will have been abandoned in 30 years' time.

After a terrible drought in 1988, people began to realise that they needed to protect the Everglades not only for the farmers, but for their own drinking water supply. A programme has now been set up to ensure that the swamps get their fair share of water and that only a limited amount of water is pumped off for drinking and irrigation.

Endangered species

Large parts of the southwestern USA were once covered in large systems of lakes. Some 100,000 years ago, the area underwent a drying-out period and pupfish, formerly

△ Alligators in the Everglades National Park, Florida, USA

widespread in the lakes, dwindled in numbers as their habitat was severely reduced. Today, the devil's hole pupfish is the world's most restricted fish. It lives in a small pool 18m below the desert floor in Nevada, USA.

The pupfish's only food are small invertebrates (animals without backbones) which feed on algae growing on a shelf of rock near the pond surface. In recent years, the pumping of underground water some distance away lowered the water level in the pool. The shelf was in danger of being exposed to the air, which would have destroyed the pupfish's food supply. Scientists studying the fish quickly built a lower shelf in the pool and the US Supreme Court ordered the pumping to be stopped. For the time being, the devil's hole pupfish is safe in its tiny home. Any further pumping of water could destroy it completely, as it seems unable to survive anywhere else.

Habitat loss is not the only reason for a species becoming endangered. In Asia, over 200 million bull frogs are killed each year to provide the food market with frogs' legs. This has led to an imbalance in the food chain in the ponds where the frogs live. It has also had another serious effect. The frogs eat malaria-carrying mosquitoes, thus acting as natural pest controllers. With fewer frogs to kill the mosquitoes, the threat of malaria is increasing.

Adult leeches feed on blood and were once widely used by doctors for blood-letting. Leeches now face another onslaught from medical science. As they feed, they produce a chemical, called hirudin, which allows blood to flow freely by preventing it from clotting. A leech can suck about four times its own weight in blood at one time, though it takes about seven months for this to be digested. By the end of this century, scientists hope to produce hirudin artificially but at present some 12,000kg of leeches are used in its manufacture each year.

Freshwater leeches live in a wide variety of habitats – in ponds, marshes and streams. The destruction of these habitats adds to the pressure already on the leeches.

A bird sanctuary in Spain

The Coto Doñana National Park in Spain is one of the world's most valuable wetlands. It is home to about 10,000 flamingoes and provides shelter for otters, lynx and imperial eagles, amongst many other animals. The Park is especially important, though, as a resting place on one of the major migration routes for birds travelling between Europe and Africa.

Despite its status as a protected area, Coto Doñana is under threat from two directions. Huge quantities of underground water are being piped off for irrigation of surrounding farmland, which is drying up the marsh land and lagoons. The increase in tourism to the area is also destroying the wetlands. Tourist hotels, golf courses and a planned beach resort will require some 12 billion litres of water a year.

The effect on the area's wildlife could be devastating. Among the 1,000 or so species of birds threatened with extinction today, many are migratory birds. They have followed the same routes for thousands of years, using the same spots to rest and feed en route. Many birds could not survive the destruction of these crucial sites.

△ The wood stork is threatened by the destruction of the Everglades.

△ Flamingoes are protected in the Coto Doñana National Park.

crustaceans – aquatic animals with a hard shell, such as shrimps and crabs.
microhabitats – a tiny living space such as that between grains of sand.
photosynthesis – the process by which plants make food, using sunlight, water, minerals and carbon dioxide.
amphibians – cold-blooded animals that live on land but breed in water.

Lakes and their wildlife

Like ponds, lakes can shrink and change. Water enters the lake through streams, rivers or rainfall. If a lake is shallow, sediment carried by a river may convert the lake into dry land, as a pond is turned into marsh.

However, major lakes such as Lake Baikal in the USSR and Lake Victoria in Africa are so deep that they do not face the problem of silting up. This fact, combined with their isolation and their great age, has led to them developing their own unique communities of animals. In fact, many lakes form quite distinctive habitats. Animals can reach them, carried by rivers, but they cannot swim out again as they are not strong enough to swim against the river currents.

Seals in Siberia

Lake Baikal in Siberia, USSR, is the deepest lake in the world. The maximum depth of its water is 1,742m. The volume of water it holds is greater than that of the five Great Lakes in North America put together.

The deeper waters of the lake are mostly lifeless. They are freezing cold, pitch black and very poor in oxygen. Because the lake is not disturbed by currents, warmer water

△ Lake Baikal, USSR

tends to lie in a layer on top. Lake Baikal is home to about 1,200 known species of animals and 500 species of plants. Over three quarters of these are found nowhere else in the world. They include molluscs and huge red and orange striped flatworms.

Among Lake Baikal's most unusual

▽ Baikal seal

△ Lake Magadi is one of the soda lakes in the Great Rift Valley in Africa.

animals is a unique mammal, the Baikal seal. It stands apart from other seals as the only freshwater seal in the world. Scientists think that the Baikal seal must be descended from the Arctic ringed seal, but that it travelled to the lake along rivers during the Ice Age, when the route from the Arctic was much shorter.

The seals feed mainly on deep-water fish. They stand at the top of a food chain which begins with a type of freshwater shrimp. Increased chemical pollution is killing the shrimp, and so threatening the seals' food supply. The seals were also once widely hunted and their numbers severely reduced. There are, today, about 70,000 seals in Lake Baikal.

Lake Baikal is part of the Baikalsky and Darguzinsky State Reserve, in the USSR. The reserve is home to over 220 species of birds and some 40 species of mammals, including the seals, reindeer and sable. However, recent industrial developments on the lake shore are increasing the risk of pollution to this unique habitat.

The great lakes of Africa

The lakes of the Great Rift Valley in Africa lie in a huge crack caused by movements of the Earth's crust millions of years ago. The valley cuts through Africa from Lebanon in the Middle East to Mozambique, extending for about 6,500km. The Great Rift lakes lie on the valley floor.

Many of the Rift lakes are rich in the mineral soda (sodium carbonate). In Lake Magadi the soda forms a crust on the lake bed as the water evaporates in the heat. Soda is used in the manufacture of glass, soap and detergents. It is one of Kenya's largest mineral exports – about half a million tonnes of soda are taken each year from Lake Magadi alone.

The concentration of soda in some of the lakes makes them uninhabitable for many forms of aquatic life. Sometimes, however, the soda in the lakes can have unexpected benefits for wildlife. Lake Nakuru in Kenya is a soda lake. Yet algae and tiny shrimps flourish in its water, providing plenty of food for the two million lesser flamingoes which

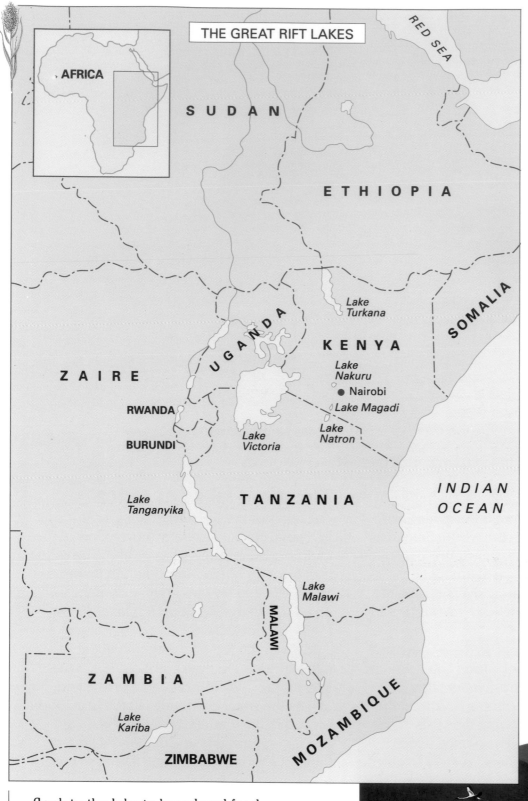

THE GREAT RIFT LAKES

AFRICA

RED SEA

SUDAN

ETHIOPIA

SOMALIA

Lake
Turkana

KENYA

UGANDA

Lake
Nakuru

● Nairobi

ZAIRE

Lake Magadi

RWANDA

Lake
Natron

BURUNDI

Lake
Victoria

TANZANIA

INDIAN
OCEAN

Lake
Tanganyika

Lake
Malawi

MALAWI

ZAMBIA

MOZAMBIQUE

Lake
Kariba

ZIMBABWE

◁ The Great Rift
lakes form two
chains. The eastern
chain contains Lake
Nakuru (see below).
Lake Tanganyika is in
the western chain.

▽ Lesser flamingoes
abound on Lake
Nakuru.

flock to the lake to breed and feed.
Flamingoes are filter feeders. They hold
their large curved beaks in the water and,
using their tongues as pistons, suck up water
and mud. The water is then pumped out of
the beak through its sieve-like edges, so that
algae and shrimps are left behind. The
flamingo's famous pink colour comes from
the food it eats. The algae contain large

32

amounts of orange-red pigments, similar to those that give carrots their colour. Without this algae flamingoes soon fade to a dull grey colour and do not breed successully. It is estimated that about 60 dry tonnes of algae are taken from Lake Nakuru every day by the flamingoes.

Hundreds of thousands of greater flamingoes favour another lake, Lake Natron, as their breeding ground. Here the levels of soda are so high as to be lethal to most other creatures. Each pair of flamingoes builds a mound-shaped mud nest on the lake shore, with a scoop in the top for the egg. The nest is usually about 30cm high, to protect it from flooding and from the intense heat of the water. In Lake Natron, this may reach a scalding 60°C.

Cichlids galore

Lake Tanganyika is the deepest lake in Africa. It has a maximum depth of about 1,400m and is thought to be the second deepest lake in the world, next to Lake Baikal. The lake covers an area larger than Belgium and is many millions of years old.

Because of its age and isolation, Lake Tanganyika, like Lake Baikal, has its own special collection of animals. Many of the lake's mussels and shrimps are unique, and about 80 per cent of its fish are found nowhere else. Among them are the cichlids – perch-like fish – which make up about two

▽ A female mouthbrooder guards her young.

thirds of all the lake's fish. Some 98 per cent of these cichlid species are found only in Lake Tanganyika.

The cichlids are best known for the care they take of their young. Most fish leave their eggs to hatch untended. Cichlids, however, take their parental responsibilities more seriously. The parents guard their eggs and once the young fish have hatched, some cichlid parents fan them to make sure they get plenty of oxygenated water.

Another group of cichlids, the mouth-brooders, are even more diligent. The eggs are fertilised, then one of the parents keeps them in its mouth for ten or so days until they hatch. Even then, the young fish stay in their parent's mouth until they have completed their development and can look after themselves. The young may make short trips outside but they are sucked back inside if danger threatens.

The people of Lake Turkana

For the people living around the Rift lakes, any change in the lakes brings a change in their lifestyles too. The Turkana live along the shores of Lake Turkana in the eastern chain of Rift lakes. The lake is 265km long and about 30km wide. It gets much of its water from the River Omo, which flows from Ethiopia.

Traditionally, the Turkana are nomads. They wandered along the valley with their herds of goats, cattle and camels, living off blood and milk from the animals. However, in the 1960s a terrible drought brought famine and the Turkana had to turn to fishing to make their living. The lake has a rich supply of fish. The Turkana had no problems in catching huge Nile perch, which can weigh up to 90kg each, and small fish, called tilapia, which are found in shallow waters. They had, though, to turn away from their ancient way of life where their status in the tribe had been determined by the size of their herds. The Turkana set up a shared storage place for the fish in one of the shore-line villages, and sent the fish by truck to large towns and cities, such as Nairobi. They prospered and began to change their lifestyle even more.

△ The Turkana dry fish taken from Lake Turkana at Ferguson's Gulf.

Now, however, their lives are having to change again. The lake is shrinking. This may be because of years of drought in Ethiopia which have dried up the River Omo. It may also be because the local climate has changed and less rain falls. One particularly good fishing spot, Ferguson's Gulf, is now dry land. You can drive over it in a car. Many of the Turkana have been forced back to their old way of life, although the lack of rainfall has much reduced the grazing land. Many were very glad to do so. Some have remained as fishermen. Others have been forced to travel to Nairobi in search of work, returning empty-handed because of the lack of jobs. No one knows how long the lake will go on shrinking, but it has already changed the Turkana's lives dramatically.

A lake in the desert

Lake Ichkeul National Park, close to the Mediterranean Sea in Tunisia, is one of the world's most important wetlands. The area comprises a lake and marshland which, together, cover nearly 130 sq km. Desert covers a large part of Tunisia. Lake Ichkeul is a permanent lake which does not dry up in the sun, which makes it a vital feeding and resting place for many migratory birds.

Lake Ichkeul is one of the top three wintering grounds for waterfowl in the western Mediterranean. The others are the Camargue in France and Coto Doñana in Spain (see page 29). In winter, up to 150,000 birds arrive at Lake Ichkeul. Among them are wigeon and coot whose breeding grounds in northern Europe and Siberia are frozen over.

Thousands of greylag geese also spend the winter here, roosting on the lake itself and feeding in the surrounding marshland. The huge rafts of pondweed which cover the lake provide food for large numbers of ducks. Herons, waders and flamingoes use the lake as a stop-over point on their way south. The nearby mountains are important breeding grounds for birds of prey.

Lake Ichkeul's survival is under threat because of the need for water in an otherwise dry area. Dams are being built on rivers to the north which divert freshwater away from the lake. However, this would upset the balance of salt water from the Mediterranean and freshwater which reach the wetlands and make them such an attractive wildlife habitat. An increase in salt water would increase the salinity of the lake to the point where its wildlife could no longer survive.

A project is now under way, involving the Tunisian Government and various conservation groups, to save the lake. They are working together to build a sluice across the river which connects the lake to the sea, to control the inflow of sea water and the outflow of freshwater. This will not only protect the environment, but provide water supplies to local people.

Lakeland specialists

The animals that live in lakes and around their edges often have special features to help them survive in this watery environment. The African jacana, for example, walks across the plants and lily pads floating on a lake's surface to catch its food of insects, small fish and seeds. It has huge feet, with toes up to 8cm long, which spread its weight evenly over the vegetation so that it does not sink into the water.

Fishing cats live in the marsh land around lakes and near rivers in many parts of Asia. The cat has slightly webbed feet and is an excellent swimmer. It perches on a rock in the water and keeps a lookout for passing fish which it scoops up with its paw.

Moose, the largest deer, live in the lakeside forests of northern Europe and North America. In summer, a moose eats over 8kg of aquatic plants, such as pondweed and bladderwort, a day, wading into the water to reach them.

The duck-billed platypus lives in streams, rivers and lakes in eastern Australia. It is one of only two types of mammal to lay eggs. Platypuses rely heavily on their sense of touch, as they close their eyes and ears underwater to stop water getting in. They eat insects, worms, shellfish and larvae.

▷ African jacana

▽ Duck-billed platypus

Lakes under threat

Many lakes face the same problems of survival as rivers and wetlands. Their water is polluted by agricultural and industrial run-off carried by rivers. Another pressure is the use of lakes for recreation. Sailing, boating, and lakeside development increase the amount of oil and rubbish dumped in the water. These factors change the lake habitat, and many animals and plants cannot adapt.

Eutrophication

The effect of fertiliser run-off (see page 10) on lakes can be disastrous. Fertilisers contain large amounts of nitrates and phosphates. If these pour into lakes they can cause **eutrophication** to take place. The nitrates and phosphates provide nourishment for algae, which grow much more rapidly than normal. Because lake water is fairly still, the algae are not flushed away and may 'bloom', forming thick green mats on the lake. These mats block sunlight from the water and plants below the surface die because they cannot photosynthesise. As the plants decay they use up the oxygen which animals need to survive.

Eutrophication is a major threat to many lakes. Among those affected by fertilisers are Lake Geneva in Switzerland and Lake Balaton in Hungary, where run-off from farms and vineyards has greatly increased the amounts of nitrates and phosphates.

Untreated sewage can also cause eutrophication. In many countries the waste is piped to treatment plants where its harmful ingredients are removed. However, some countries pump raw sewage straight into the sea, and into rivers and lakes.

Eutrophication is a particular problem in countries which dispose of large amounts of detergents with their sewage waste. In Japan, many lakes are dying because of the phosphates discharged into them from heavy-duty, synthetic detergents.

Various measures can be taken to reduce

△ Mats of green algae cover a pond.

▽ Lack of oxygen has killed these bream.

the impact of fertilisers and sewage waste on our lakes. Larger amounts of phosphates could be removed from sewage at treatment plants, and treatment plants could be built where none exist.

There is also pressure on farmers to break away from modern methods of farming and adopt **organic farming** methods which work with nature, not against it. Some farmers now do farm organically, using organic waste such as animal manure,

△ The city of Toronto is on the shores of Lake Ontario, one of the five Great Lakes.

instead of chemicals. They also use crop rotation. Several different crops are grown in a field over a period of four to five years. Crops which put nutrients into the soil are alternated with crops which remove them.

Toxic soup

The Great Lakes are a group of five connected lakes on the border of Canada and the USA. Together, the five – Superior, Michigan, Erie, Huron and Ontario – cover an area of about 246,000 sq km. Some of the world's top industrial cities, such as Chicago and Detroit, lie on the lake shores.

The St Lawrence River connects the Great Lakes to the Atlantic Ocean. The river flows from Lake Ontario to the Gulf of St Lawrence. Part of the river has been turned into a canal and it now forms a major shipping route into North America. Over the past 30 years, industries on its banks and in the area around the Great Lakes have poured in so many toxic chemicals, including lethal PCBs, that its water is now unsafe for fish,

animals and people for much of its length. Such huge amounts of sewage and agricultural and industrial waste have been discharged into Lake Erie, for example, that the lake is biologically dead. Despite the passing of a Clean Water Act in 1972 in the USA, fish suffering from various liver and skin cancers are still being found in the Great Lakes.

The plight of the belugas

Scientists are now deeply concerned about the plight of a group of beluga whales which live around the St Lawrence estuary. Dead whales are being washed up at the rate of about one a month. They are so full of poisonous chemicals that they are now classified as toxic waste. Unless something is done to clean up the whole lake and river system, this group of whales could quickly become extinct. Although they are found elsewhere, this group is of particular interest. It has survived in isolation in this area since the Ice Age.

△ Thousands of lakes in Norway (above) and Sweden are affected by acid rain.

Acid rain

Lakes and rivers in more than 20 industrialised countries are now affected by rain as acidic as vinegar. Acid rain is caused by fumes and gas from factory chimneys and car exhausts rising into the air. Many of these fumes come from burning fossil fuel, such as coal. They contain large amounts of sulphur dioxide gas. Car exhaust fumes contain large amounts of nitrogen oxide gas. Worldwide, over 130 tonnes of man-made sulphur dioxide and about 36 million tonnes of nitrogen oxide are discharged into the air each year. High up in the atmosphere, these gases react with the water in the water cycle and with sunlight to form weak solutions of sulphuric and nitric acid. This falls to Earth as acid rain.

Acid rain kills fish by making active poisonous metals such as aluminium that are in the water, or by washing them from the soil into the lake. In the water, the poisons clog fishes' gills so they suffocate.

The wind can carry pollutants over 2,000km before they fall as rain. Canada's lakes are affected by acid rain which originates in the USA. Great Britain produces the pollutants that fall over Scandinavia. In Sweden, one of the countries with the best

pollution records, about 90,000 lakes are too acidic to support life. Another 38,000 are in danger. By 1982, 1,750 Norwegian lakes had lost all their fish.

Some power stations are already being fitted with filters which remove sulphur. Catalytic converters on car exhausts make most of the poisonous gases harmless. In 1987, many countries signed an agreement to join the '30 per cent Club'. They agreed to cut the amount of sulphur produced in 1980 by at least 30 per cent by 1993. In the longer term, though, alternative forms of energy, such as solar, wind and water power, may offer the best and cleanest solutions.

For the present, countries such as Sweden are trying to clean up their polluted lakes. Scientists use a process known as 'liming' to remove the acid. The lakes are spread with powdered limestone, which is an alkaline and so it neutralises the acid. The disadvantage of this solution is that lakes need to be sprayed often, which is time-consuming. Another problem is that the addition of lime changes the chemical content of the water. This can cause further damage to wildlife if the lake's plants and animals cannot adapt to the new type of environment.

Water hyacinth – good or bad?

The water hyacinth, a type of water fern, can be a natural threat to the health of rivers and lakes. It spreads very quickly, clogging the water, and can be toxic to fish. It is usually considered a harmful weed but studies in Florida, USA, have found a potential use for the fern, as a pollution filter. The plant can absorb nitrates and phosphates from the water and so prevent eutrophication. It can also remove huge quantities of the poisonous metal, lead, in a very short time. If the plant's growth can be controlled to prevent clogging, it could be used as a natural way of reducing pollution in badly affected lakes.

◁ A helicopter sprays powdered limestone over a lake in Sweden.

The Ramsar Convention

International pressure to protect lakes and wetlands led to the Ramsar Convention coming into force in 1975 (see page 5). Ramsar aims to encourage countries to halt the destruction of these important ecosystems. Each country that signs the agreement has to propose at least one wetland for inclusion on a world list, and pledge to work for its conservation. In 1990, about 52 countries had signed and the list included over 460 wetlands. However, many countries with important wetlands have still to be persuaded to join. The importance of wetlands was initially judged by their value to waterfowl. This has now been widened to include a whole range of plants and animals, and the value of wetlands to local communities for fishing, collecting firewood and plants, and drinking water supplies.

eutrophication – the process by which water is deprived of oxygen by the rapid growth of algae on its surface.
organic farming – farming without chemicals such as pesticides.

Looking ahead

Freshwater is an essential part of our everyday lives. We drink it, cook and wash in it. In countries where water is plentiful, each person uses over 500 litres of water every day. Industry, too, uses huge quantities of water. The energy contained in running water provides us with power, and rivers and lakes are the focus of many leisure activities such as swimming, sailing and fishing. These are just a very few of the reasons why we should look after our freshwater supply before it becomes too contaminated to use.

Water for life

Water is essential to living things. We need to take in at least two litres of water a day (in food as well as drinks) in order to survive. For many of us, we just turn on the tap and water comes out. But in many of the poorer parts of the world, people have to find water where they can, often walking for up to four hours a day to collect their precious supply. In such cases, people may use only two and a half litres of water a day, close to the lowest limit necessary to life. While countries like Iceland have far more water than they need, about two billion people around the world suffer long-term water shortages.

The world's use of water has more than tripled in the last 40 years. About half of the freshwater used in developed countries such as the USA is used by industry. In poorer countries such as India, over 90 per cent of the freshwater is used for irrigation and growing food.

In many African and Asian countries, the quality of drinking water is very poor. It has to be taken from whatever source is available, often contaminated ponds or rivers. In Ethiopia, over 90 per cent of people do not have clean water.

The effect on people's health of dirty water can be devastating. At least 25,000 people die every day from using dirty water, making

it one of the world's greatest killers. Waterborne diseases, such as diarrhoea and cholera, are among the worst offenders. They are caused by germs which breed in water containing human waste. Over half the people who die of diarrhoea could be saved if they had adequate sanitation and clean, safe water.

Although the problem of dirty water is most acute in the world's poorer countries, it is also a threat to people in richer countries, despite the treatment and cleaning of water in sewage plants and water works. In Sweden and Norway, drinking water is affected by acid rain (see page 38). Here it has been linked with a rise in the number of people suffering from Alzheimer's disease, a form of senile dementia. This illness is thought to be linked with high levels of aluminium, released from the water by the acid rain, affecting the brain.

In 1980 the United Nations launched the International Drinking Water Supply and Sanitation Decade. Their slogan was 'Clean water and adequate sanitation for all by the year 1990'. For the first three years, the campaign proved very successful. Better sanitation was provided for about 150 million people and clean drinking water for about 350 million.

Today however, there are still millions of people without proper sanitation or safe drinking water. Although many governments, including that in India, increased the amount they spent on sanitation, the campaign's progress gradually slowed down. Without sufficient overseas aid, budgets remained low and could not meet the enormous need in many countries.

Acorn option

In Korea, scientists are working on an ingenious solution to the country's river pollution problems. Acorns are a traditional food in Korea. They are made into a brown, jelly-like cake. Scientists think that acorns may prove the key ingredient in cleaning up rivers heavily contaminated by heavy metals from industry.

Acorns contain tannic acid and 'acornic' acid. Acornic acid seems to be able to remove the metals from the water. They sink to the bottom and can be filtered off. In water treated with acornic acid, the amount of uranium had been reduced to 0.1 parts per 1,000 of water. Water treated traditionally still had 5 parts of uranium per 1,000. Scientists estimate that 1kg of acorns could remove the poisonous waste from 3.5 tonnes of water.

The 'acorn option' is still in its experimental stage and scientists are hoping to open a pilot plant soon to produce acornic acid. They are working on finding the chemical structure of the acid, so it can be produced synthetically and in large quantities. This would also reduce potential damage to the oak forests.

▽ Women in Rajasthan, in India, have to carry water to their village.

Water for power

Flowing freshwater contains huge amounts of energy, which can be converted into electricity. People harnessed this power many hundreds of years ago to turn water mills to grind corn. About a fifth of the world's electricity is now supplied by hydroelectric power stations. Dams are constructed across rivers to form a reservoir and create a head of water (the distance between the water source and the turbines). The higher the head of water, the greater the water pressure. This turns the blades of turbines, sometimes built in the base of the dam, which generate electricity. Dams are also built to harness river water for irrigation and to help control flooding.

With the world's increasing use of, and therefore need of, energy, hydroelectric power seems a promising source. However, the building of large hydroelectric dams causes many environmental problems. The huge Aswan Dam on the River Nile holds back the river water in a huge reservoir, Lake Nasser. Mud that would normally fertilise the river delta is now silting up the lake (see page 8). Lake Mead, on the Colorado River in the USA, has been created by the building of the massive Hoover Dam. In less than 400 years' time, though, sediment deposited by the river will have silted up the lake completely.

Another worrying aspect of large hydroelectric dams and the filling of their reservoirs is the possibility of earth tremors caused by the added pressure they put on the Earth's crust. Hundreds of earth tremors were felt in the area after Lake Mead was filled with water, and following the construction of the Kariba Dam in Zimbabwe (see map on page 32).

Large dams also cause social problems. Up to one million people may have to be resettled if the plan to build the Three Gorges Dam on the Yangtze River, China, goes ahead. Their villages and homes will be destroyed to clear the areas for building.

▽ A lake has been created by the building of the Hoover Dam in Nevada, USA.

△ This village sits on an island of reeds in Lake Titicaca (inset).

Tidal power

Electricity can also be produced from the energy created by the rising and falling of tides in a river estuary. A dam, or barrage, is built across the river mouth. The world's largest tidal barrage was built across the estuary of the River Rance, in France, in 1966. The dam is 750m long. It has 24 tunnels along its length, each containing a turbine. The turbine blades can be reversed, so that energy can be collected both when the tide is going out and when it is coming in. The barrage can generate about 240 megawatts of electricity. This source of power may well become more widespread in the future, though great care will have to be taken to ensure that the wildlife of river estuaries is not disturbed.

People and water

In many parts of the world, water is not only important for drinking and power. For some people, their whole way of life depends on water, whether in lakes, rivers, ponds or swamps. Lake Titicaca is the world's highest large lake. It is about 4,000m up in the Andes mountains, on the border between Bolivia and Peru. The lake has been a centre of South American Indian life since the time of the Incas, over 1,000 years ago.

The lake is still densely populated and its wildlife is still vital to its people. Thick mats of totora reeds form large, floating islands on the lake. The people live on these islands and also use the reeds for building huts and boats and making baskets to use and sell. Submerged aquatic plants, called yacco, are harvested and fed to vicuna and cattle that graze at the edges of the lake. The Indians' dependence on the lake is shown by the fact that they take about 6,000 tonnes of fish from the lake each year.

Lake plants also play a vital part on the lives of people living around Lake Texcoco in Mexico. Since Aztec times, people have collected a type of alga, called spirulina, which grows on the surface of the lake.

The alga is packed with protein and the Aztecs used to make it into biscuits. Today, the alga is manufactured commercially in factories in Mexico and California. One factory, near to the lake, produces five tonnes of spirulina a day. At the moment it is used for animal feed, but it may be able to be used to make a kind of milk and to replace meat in vegetarian soups.

Water is a precious resource and we all need to make an effort to look after it. Even on a domestic level we can help improve the quality of our water, by using biodegradable detergents (which break down naturally) and household cleaners that contain smaller amounts of harmful ingredients (such as bleaches that do not rely heavily on chlorine). It is not only animals and plants that stand to lose if our water is contaminated. None of us will benefit from drinking dirty water.

Fortunately, many governments and conservation groups are realising the danger our water is in. With regular monitoring of rivers, legislation to reduce the amount of waste dumped in rivers and lakes, and organisations such as Ramsar, our freshwater may, one day soon, be fresh again and the natural balance of freshwater habitats all over the world may be restored.

▽ Rivers in Bhutan are clean because there is so little industry in the country.

44